# THE FIVE KEYS TO A SUCCESSFUL RELATIONSHIP

## A Guide To Understanding Relationships

N. J. DiCarlo

# FOREWORD

To my family, friends, and co-workers. For without you, I would not have made it this far in my life. I would not know what is needed in a relationship had it not been for the challenging times we've had together. I owe everyone one of you my life for teaching me the things I know now.

Never give up.
Never settle.

N.J. DiCarlo

# CONTENTS

Title Page

Copyright

Foreword

Introduction     1

Trust Starts with You     9

Being Honest and True     16

You Have to Talk     23

Bargaining in Life     31

Love is All You Need     37

Conclusion     41

About The Author     45

# INTRODUCTION

Thanks for picking this book as you further your life's goals and ambitions. I'm sure by now you are wondering who the writer of this book is. I am N.J. DiCarlo, from a small town in Missouri that joined the Army as a young age and has traveled all over the continental U.S. I built many relationships along my journey.

My first serious employment with the Army required me to trust, communicate, and be honest. Drill instructors have a tough job; training new recruits that have no idea what they are doing in terms of military basics. In South Carolina at Fort Jackson, I learned a great deal of what an employment relationship needs to not only enjoy what you do, but also to have a successful venture. Throughout my short stint in the military, due to suffering injuries, I met hundreds of people. People that did not quite understand how to have working relationships or even intimate relationships with others. It was definitely not my responsibiity to tell them how to live their lives and what to do with those relationships. Right now, though, I almost wish I could have at least spoke to them on what I know now. Maybe they would still have those relationships. Or they might be better off without those relationships. No job should require you to hurt others in order to succeed, but this was the thought process of many in the military. Thankfully, people are waking up and speaking up about these certain individuals.

No one deserves to be treated any differently based solely on a demographic. First and foremost treat others how you would want to be treated. Have we lost our humanity? Or is it selfishness that has infested the hearts and minds of millions of people worldwide?

I was engaged with my beautiful fiancé. When we first met, our communication skills were terrible. She is from the Philippines and I am from the United States. The language barrier was tough to break down. She had this stigma about American white males; they are only about sex and will use you. Sure, there are those that do that no matter their skin tone, but it is not everyone and certainly not me. We had to literally take baby steps in our relationship. One time she broke up with me because of her racist friends.

This is one thing you must do, DO NOT LISTEN TO THOSE FRIENDS. Especially if they are racist. Sometimes our friends are like flies. They fly around us to get a reaction and bother us so they can feel better about themselves. There is no need for friends like that in your life. Besides her friends, we have had our moments and break-ups. Through it all, she was my rock. Believe it or not, when we first dated, it was my first intimate relationship that goes beyond just sex. A deeper relationship that dives into the heart and soul. I have always believed that in an intimate relationship sex was just a bonus. More on that later. I will say this, it is not the 'make or break it' in a relationship.

What breaks the relationship normally deals with the 5 keys you will learn more about. But if you are reading this, you are probably wondering: "What does this 28-year-old man know about relationships?" I know plenty from my own experiences. It's not a bad thing if you have the slightest idea what is required in a realtionship. Relationships are very fragile, intricately designed things in life. It can take months or even years to establish a relationship with another human being. But I will tell you, no matter who you are with, you can be successful as long as you want it. Whether you want a better relationship with a friend, coworker, mother, father, sister, brother, or even a lover, the information I have written for you will be supremely helpful. I have some easy to understand advice that will make these relationships prosper for you and other people involved. Now, I am by no means an expert, nor do I have the education to prove that I know what I am talking about. What I do have though, is experience. With experience comes pain, heartache, depression, anxiety, and loneliness. I am not much of a cupid. Never have really been a romantic either. It does not stop me from being the best decent person I can be though. That is what most people look for in a friend, lover, or coworker; someone that is a decent human being.

No one is perfect, no one. Not even I am perfect. We all have our faults and weaknesses. Growing up, I lived in my grandmother's house for the most part. After having this emotional stress of not having a complete family in my life, I went out into a neighbor's field behind my house and screamed at the top of my lungs. An old frail woman came out of her house and motioned me to come to her. She did not ask me why I was screaming or even tell me to shut up. She took me in to sit down and have a soda. This is what really opened my mind on understanding how relationships work. Toni Bess was her name, she passed not more than a few years ago now. Through our relationship as friends, I learned a lot from her. She taught me how to communicate properly and how to pick good friends. I ended up working for her as much as I could. She was literally my first employer. She was the nicest person you would ever see, and people often took advantage of that trait. I could not though, because she showed me compassion and understanding when I needed it the most. On top of that, taking advantage of people is immoral. She was the kind of person you want in your life. I am glad she was in mine.

After giving you some insight on myself, you are

probably still skeptical. I get it, I would be too. Just hear me out though. Ever since I figured out what makes a relationship really work, it has done wonders for me in almost every aspect of my life. Sure, there were times where my mouth would actually ruin my relationships, but I was able to rebuild them by using 5 simple keys. No, not keys that go on your keychain. These keys are the essentials for building and maintaining relationships. I learned each one at a different stage in my life. It does take time to really understand how life and relationships work. The foundation is what I will be going over with you. That is why I decided to write this book so that in no time, you too, will be able to have relationships that last forever.

As long as you are willing to accept what I am about to give to you and use it, your relationships will benefit from this knowledge that I will share with you. If you take the time to read this, then you can repair and build any relationship in your life.

What are the Five Keys of a Successful Relationship? Okay, you have made it this far and really want to learn. I could not be more ecstatic with your decision. I want to break this down for you. There are five essential keys to a successful relationship. As I mentioned earlier, these relationships have no boundaries in where they lay or even how you implement them, just as long as you utilize them constantly, together. One thing is a must that will be explained as we go further into these keys; you must first start with yourself. Working with an active relationship is fine, but if you do not start the relationship with yourself, how do you imagine having one with another human being will turn out?

Without further delay, let us begin our journey. We have five keys, and those five keys are essential with every relationship we have. Just take a look at this handy image:

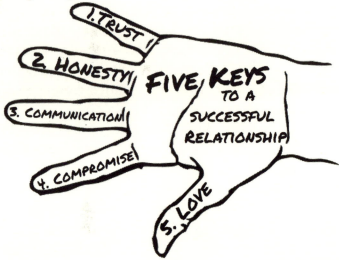

In order, we have trust, honesty, communication, compromise, and love. Each one is a different function with any relationship, and you cannot have one without the other. I say this because it is true. Have you ever tried to love someone without trusting them? How about communicating without being honest? Or what about being able to agree on a compromise without having communication? Everything we do in life falls on these basic understandings of what a relationship is supposed to be.

As you learn, this path will help you build and re-build relationships with those that you care about, even the most important one with yourself.

Every relationship starts with communication. Talking to another person to get to know them is critical. Know who they are, what they do, how they treat others is necessary in knowing if that person qualifies to be in your life. You can be picky about this. You need to be picky about this. There is nothing worse than having a toxic friend or partner in your life. It will not be a positive experience, and you will be miserable. Take time in building relationships. There is not a race to see how many friends you can have in your life.

If you are young, you will see as you age, most of your friends you made in high school will no longer be around. They have moved on and so should you. Finding a casual relationship is the tricky part. Most people do not show their true colors until you get really comfortable with their existence. When that happens, you have to end that relationship. If that person is able to change, let them change without you. If you stay, that person will be like a leach and not let go. It is better to let go than to stay around a toxic person. They will only bring you down to their level where you too will be miserable. The majority of people look for others that relate to them on a personal level. You will find that everyone is relatable to a certain extent. Pretty simple, right?

To understand this process, you first need to understand that the road can be easy if you let it, otherwise you will find that fighting against it will ruin the road and make it that much more difficult to drive on. Through each step you will either learn or realize that most of the issues happen due our inability to maintain order. Now, order is not about law, it is more about controlling our emotions and actions. Each step, you will begin to see this connection as long as you stick with it. Relationships, in the beginning, are fragile and any wrongdoing or misstep can turn it into a broken mess. But, if you apply what you will learn and understand in this very book, you can avoid that mess. You may even be able to clean up prior messes from mistakes you may have made. Our first task is to trust. Let us dive right on into it.

# TRUST STARTS
# WITH YOU

**W**hen most people think about trust, it is this small thing when in reality it is the exact opposite. It is probably the most important key out of all of them, at least in the beginning. Trust is also very fragile. One misdeed can ruin the trust in a relationship within a single second. Being able to rely on people is part of society as a whole. Think about it, when we elect our leaders, we must have a sense of trust in their ability to do what is right and listen to those that voted for them.

You have to start right where it matters most. Yourself! If you think about it, *do you trust yourself*?

Really think about it. You have to, right? I mean if you don't you wouldn't be where you are today. I am trusting in my ability to write this book so that you can learn about how to have a successful relationship. Trusting oneself is very important in this process. Everything we do in life, we have to believe in ourselves, that we will do what is right and succeed for our own sake.

If you do not trust yourself right now, do not worry, you are not alone in this effort. Normally, we learn to trust ourselves as we mature and grow up. Sometimes this process is interrupted due to outside forces. Parents' divorce, moving around too much, loosing friends, even puberty has an effect.

These changes do not define you. I will tell you right now, when my parents divorced, the first time, I thought I was the issue. I thought that I made them fall out of love. Never ever think this way. Your parents' decisions have nothing to do with you when it comes to their own relationship. That is the first thing I had to learn, especially when they decided to give it another try only to end up divorcing again. One time, I asked my mother why they even got back together if she was not in love with my father anymore. Her answer: we did it for you and your sister. This is never a good reason to get back together with an ex-relationship, even if you have kids together. A move like this only puts more stress in the household. If you and your partner broke up, there is a reason for it; there was a breakdown in the relationship that is detailed somewhere along the lines

I discuss within this book. You will see it when we get there. It'll feel like a light buble lit up in your head, an epiphany as they call it. It could even be trust.

When I met my partner, six years ago, she did not know me, and I did not know her. It took many dates and months to be able to trust myself with her and her with me. She has four kids, and at the time they were all under 11 years old. Why would she trust me with them? I look back and do not blame her for not wanting me to see them the first time we dated. A parent should protect their kids no matter what, especially in the beginning of a relationship. Trust takes time to build a rapport. The worst thing about trust is that it can easily be broken. You see, my partner at the time, seen me as another man just looking for sex. That was far from the truth. I even told her this, but still she did not trust me and really had no reason to either. You cannot trust just words, wholeheartedly. Actions speak louder than words, and by my actions she slowly started to trust me.

I must be honest with you; I did lose her trust completely one time. When I look back, I feel that hiding it was not the best thing to do. I, like everyone else are curious creatures. We tend to want to know about taboos and things that relate to sexual desires. Pornography was my problem. I was addicted. To the point where it almost destroyed the most important relationship in my life.

I will not make any excuses. I hide it because I

was ashamed of this addiction. I ventured so far into pornography that I could not get myself out of it. But once she found out, this woke me up. She wanted to leave me. I hurt her so much. She felt that she was not good enough to be with me. That she did not have what I wanted. The addiction was so trivial that I completely disregarded how she felt. I will say this, pornography can and will destroy any intimate relationship you have if that other person is not comfortable with it. From that moment, I decided that I would need to really work on myself. I would find myself drifting off in thought and boom watching pornography again, and again. It has taken me quite some time to break my old habits. Even today, I still struggle with it, but I am more aware of triggers as well as how to control my mind.

Pornography is the least of your worries if your partner is okay with it. But you have to really make sure it does not get out of hand. Jealously can infest itself if you rely too much on pornography. The intimacy in your relationship can lose that spark it once had. I have always said this: sex is important for mainly 2 things: creation and intimacy, but it is not the end-all-be-all for we do not thrive on sex as humans. When we allow pornography to run our lives, it tends to ruin the intimacy. I am not saying that you cannot explore in the bedroom, just make sure that you and your partner are comfortable with it prior to making a decision and always use moderation. Talk with your partner and set ground-rules.

Within one of my relationships, I had lost trust in my cousin.

I will not name the individual, but I will say what caused this loss in trust. I worked for a neighbor when I was younger, and my cousin joined me in helping just to make a few extra dollars. The neighbor was a great and strong, independent, and elderly woman. We both worked for her for a year, until my cousin not only betrayed her but betrayed me as well.

My cousin began to steal from her and take her vehicle on joy rides, which is a big mistake. She had only one car and if that car somehow got into an accident, she would not have been able to afford a new one. When I found out about my cousin stealing from her, I lost trust because I thought I could trust him in helping out the one woman that helped me when I was in a difficult place in my life. I blamed myself for allowing this amazing woman to be used for his monetary gain. I took it out on myself. I should have known; I should have been there to make sure she was getting what she needed from the store instead of being out with my friends. But it was not my fault entirely. I could not place this blame on myself. Sure, I allowed my cousin to get close to my neighbor, but she also took the chance herself in allowing my cousin to get her groceries for her. She caught on pretty quickly though. She was smart and figured it out. My cousin was never allowed to even visit her again.

The actions we take have only two outcomes:

positive or negative. My cousin's decisions were negative and selfish. That is why the relationship ended with my cousin. Selfishness is a terrible trait to have. Being selfish means, you do not care for others, which means you cannot have a relationship with anyone. It was my cousin's decision to treat her wrongfully, and it was only my cousin that suffered the consequences.

By our decision making, we must conclude that is not just about self. A positive outcome normally is positive for most people. Gaining trust is an important step that must not be taken lightly.

A negative outcome only profits one persona and ends with consequences. Trusting in someone is difficult to begin with. You need to build a rapport with someone before you can truly trust them completely. This is how relationships work. You strike up a conversation, you begin to learn about an individual and you test their ability to be trusted. Vice versa. If the simplest tasks show that you cannot trust them, then you probably should not trust them with a relationship. Vice versa. If you understand this and agree with it I want to repeat this phrase:

*I (your name), do trust myself. I can trust that I will make positive decisions that do not just profit myself but others too. I will always work on trusting others and know that it takes time to build trust with others as well.*

If you can say and do this, then there is no telling

how many successful relationships you can begin to have.

# BEING HONEST
# AND TRUE

HONESTY

Honesty is a must-have key in everything we do in life. You can lie as much as you want, but lying will get you nowhere fast. When you lie, you have to lie to cover that lie up and it turns into this monstrosity that ruins your outlook on life as well as your relationships with others. Honesty is simple in terms of when to be honest. Upfront is always the best scenario. Being honest starts with you.

You have to start being honest with yourself. If you are miserable at a job and you keep working there, you are not being honest with your work ethic. It may be a dead-end job and a job that you do not find enjoyment, but you must be honest with yourself. Do you really want to work there the rest of your life? If not, you have to decide now what you really want to do in life and go for it. Waiting for the right time will never come when you want it to. This is why you must act upon it now. Even in relationships you have to do the same thing.

When you are miserable with a relationship and you just stick it out because you do not want to hurt the other person, you are lying to yourself. How? You want to believe that the person that is manipulating you has good in them. Or when they use you but do not reward you in return; both of these are terrible and should not be accepted. A simple reward is just a thank-you in the least of terms. It is not something fancy like payment or gifts, a thank-you is a sign of gratitude that gives insight that the other person cares about your existence and the work you put into something. By allowing someone to continue to treat you otherwise, you are not being honest with yourself or even them. Sometimes you have to put your foot down and either walk away or casually confront them about the issue.

Now, if you look at how we are raised, for the most part, we have all been lied to by our parents. Especially when it comes to holidays. Parents lie to us to manipulate us. Why we, as a society, have allowed to continue is beyond me, but all it takes is a single person to change that. But you should also not lie to your own children, even if it is for pure amusement. Amusement which can be equated to torture. Santa Claus is not real, the Easter bunny is not real, the great feast between the pilgrims and Native Americans never happened. These are lies and manipulate not only history but our own lives. Kids should not be subjected to this kind of manipulation. It is okay to celebrate, but it is better to tell the truth. Kids will behave better when we are honest with them. Being honest with them also shows the importance of this value and in turn they will also be honest with you. Even when kids ask tons of questions, if you do not know the answer just simply say you do not know. Making up a lie to cover up not knowing an answer only shows arrogance and that you do not care enough to either look it up or say you do not know.

In my relationship, my partner lied to me about her own kids. On our first date I asked if she had any kids. I was 21 and she was 26 for context. Most women have never thought about not having kids, even though there are women out there that do not have kids at that age. It's more a personal choice in life and all about timing.

I figured I would ask her how many children she had, just to prepare my mentality on how to properly act and be a role model for them. She told me she had 10, yes 10 kids! At this moment I knew it was a lie. 26 years old with 10 kids? Impossible! I mean she could not have had that many kids within even 10 years. I mean, there are women that have done it but I still had my doubts with how she nonchallantly threw it in a sentence. I asked for further details and she answered saying she had 4 of her own and 6 kids she adopted. Now, I am no wizard of knowledge, but seeing that she worked at a minimum wage job, the math didn't add up. How could someone with only one job be able to afford living with 10 kids? I gave her some time before I revisited this topic for further discussion. Later on, she would tell me she did not actually have 10 kids but just 4. Apparently, she was just testing me on if I would be afraid enough to leave her and never speak to her again. As if having 10 kids wouldn't scare me? Be as it may, it did not really bother me, but it was a moment of make it or break it for others.

As a kid growing up in a single-family home with my mom and sister, we moved around a bit. When I was in first grade we moved to a neighboring town where my mom found a job as a janitor at a local school. While attending school, I remember becoming lazy with some homework. Spelling to be exact. Imagine how far I have come now becoming a writer. Don't get me wrong, but I think any kid would do this presenting the opportunity for a reward. The reward for correctly spelling every word on a test would be a handful of candy. Now this candy was just like M&M's, just an off brand, located in the principal's office area. I began to cheat after finding this out. I passed about 5 tests in a row and got candy every single time. I was lying to myself at a very young age. This is usually normal for most kids. Not cheating but lying to themselves. I did not believe I could pass the test without cheating. Did I know it was wrong? Yes, I sure did. I would hide the answers in my desk, you know those desks with a lid.

I would patiently wait for the teacher to call out the next word and wait for her to look someplace else and then as quietly as possible slip that sheet of paper to where I could see and quickly write the word on the test page. I was super nervous the first 2 times. Who wouldn't be? Cheating was against the rules because you do not push yourself to retain that knowledge. A couple weeks would go by and I began to get lazy. I think my teacher, Mrs. White, was catching on as well. By the fifth week, she caught me, and I was sent to the principal's office straight away. Now, at this moment I was severely afraid of the consequences. Which is a normal feeling for anyone. One moment I was eating candy, the next moment I was pulling down my pants to get a spanking from the principal with a wooden paddle. That event forged a stain in my memory. Because when I got home, I also got another spanking from my mother. An unorthodox method of punishment compared to today's standards. I learned my lesson that day. I never cheated on a test again. I pushed myself to learn more and memorize as much as I could. This is relatable to adults as well.

Everything we do in life has consequences, just like I talked about with trust. Good and bad. When we lie, it is only a matter of time before the consequences catch up with us. It may not be immediately but *trust* me, the consequences always catch up with us eventually. One thing I want to revisit is adults lying to their kids. I am not trying to tell you how to raise your own children but think about what you are teaching them. You are lying to them and saying it is okay to lie. You may be wondering, how am I lying to my kids? Have you ever told your kids that the tooth fairy is real, Santa Claus, Easter bunny, or even other fairy-tale creatures? These are lies, not very good ones, but lies, nonetheless. This sets up a precedent for the habits your own kids will have. You tell them if they misbehave, they will not get presents and such.

You are literally telling them that they should be afraid to tell the truth if it reveals that what they may have done was wrong. I think for the sake of our children, we should start being honest with them and that starts with the simple things like holidays. By doing this, it teaches kids that telling the truth the first time will reduce the consequences rather than them hiding it. We have all heard that we should teach a child in the ways they should grow up to become. It starts with telling them the truth and raising them to be honest.

Through all of this, I hope you understand the importance of being honest with yourself and those you care about around your life. Honesty begets trust and vice versa. People are more likely to be honest with you if they can trust that you will be honest with them as well. Be honest with yourself first and work on being honest with others second. If you cannot be honest with yourself on your own circumstances, then you will not be able to trust yourself to be honest with others. Do you see how that works? It may be a difficult challenge at first because we are all brought up a certain way due to the outside forces in our environments, but I am positive you can do it.

Repeat this if you believe in yourself:

*I (your name), will be honest with myself and my relationships with others in order to garner a stronger sense of trust between myself and others. I will overcome my fear of consequences to mitigate others from being hurt.*

If you can do that, then you are appropriately repairing your relationships from damage that can be avoided. Congratulations! Now we must talk about another important aspect of relationships: communication.

# YOU HAVE
# TO TALK

An issue I know that most people will deny is that they do not talk enough in a relationship. Most people will deny because they think talking about ordinary-everyday happenings is enough. How was work? How was school today? What did you learn? These questions are basic and do not create meaningful discussions. Sure, it is communication, but it is in a manner that does not dive deep into the psyche where the emotions and pain lives.

Communication with anyone is crucial. Every civilization was build upon the foundation of communication. Without it, you cannot trust people and hope for honesty in any discussion. Think about it like a trade deal. With any government in talks with another country, a trade deal needs communication in order to even develop. This is exactly how relationships work as well. You and the other person in the relationship must dig into what makes that relationship viable.

Are you both there for each other in times of need? Do either of you provide support for the other? What is the purpose of the relationship? Why do you want to be with the other person? Why is it important? These questions are important to understand how to move forward in the communication process.

If you have a friendship most of the relationship is spent in communication. This communication is basically talking to someone about problems or persistent roadblocks outside of the friendship. Most people utilize friends as a buffer to help with other relationships. This is not a terrible thing, but it can also create problems due to an outside force acting upon a subject that the person may not understand. The best thing to do if you have a problem is to talk directly to the person you have a problem with. It is never a good idea to talk to another person that may not be a viable fix to the problem when they are not part of the problem in the first place.

Now, I have had many people come to me directly with their problems. That is okay, there's nothing wrong with that. But the issue is that some people take it upon themselves to intervene and solve the issue. That is not okay. The best thing to do is to advise people. Never attempt to solve the issue unless it is requested, and you can diffuse the situation without making it worse. When someone comes to me, I often give them advise on how to handle a problem. Most often, I cannot solve the problem but I know how to handle problems. I solve my own problems, not other people's problems. A problem needs to be solved by the individuals that are within the boundaries of that problem. It would be saying $2+2=4$ and not following the rules of simple arithmetic. If I were to input any other number in there that was not a negative number, then the answer would not be 4. Plus, you really don't want a negative number to be involved in a relationship.

That negative number is anyone that gives advice and attempts to solve it. It complicates the problem. Most of the time these complications can lead to another problem and then it ruins the relationship of anyone involved.

In order to fix the problem in a relationship on your own you need to start talking to whomever is involved with the problem. I cannot stress this enough when you communicate it must be with honesty! By being dishonest you are simple complicating the problem like I mentioned above. Start the conversation with trust and honesty. From there you can begin to figure out what the underlying issue is within the problem. Majority of the time it is due to not communicating in the first place.

Take for instance my own story. In the beginning of my relationship with my partner we had a language barrier. She is Filipino and I am an American. She knew English but there were some common misconceptions on the translation of certain phrases. As we grew, within our relationship, we still had insecurity. Insecurity usually lies within a past relationship.

My partner had an abusive relationship prior to being with me and this set her mind to think that every man is the same. Obviously, this is not true, but for her at the time is was. She never really opened up about it until it came to a boiling point within our relationship. I am the type of man that is friendly with most people. I have more female friends than I do male friends. It mainly goes back to my childhood; I lived in a house with my grandmother, mother, sister, and a female cousin. Pretty sure you can see why I am more inclined to understanding women better than men. My father was never there, and even to this day I rarely talk to him. Now, with my partner, her insecurity really took a toll on our relationship. She never discussed the insecurity, nor did she ever mention her past. She would keep everything interally and leave me out to dry.

This presented two problems that I was completely unaware of at first, but I would soon figure out when that insecurity would seep into my relationships with my friends. She would text me constantly, asking me where I am at, who I am with, and if there are any women with me. That last one raised a huge red flag. I mean, who asks that kind of specific question if they trust you?

The red flag began to create a crack in our relationship. I began to question myself, thinking that I was the problem. This effected my self-esteem and in turn effected my communication and honesty. Why would it do any of that, you may ask. Simply put, if I felt that I was the problem, why would I tell her if there were any women around me? Why would I communicate to her that I was going somewhere with friends? I realized that her insecurities were affecting my ability to be the person she needed me to be. Eventually I stopped having friends in real life. Most friends that I interacted with were online.

One day, I finally had enough of not understanding why she had these insecurities. I did not go to her in anger. Anger is an emotion that clouds good judgement and prohibits productive communication. I had to go to her with a neutral mindset. The communication began with blaming which turned to arguing. We began to blame the other person for the problem. Which is true in turn, but it is not what created the problem in the first place. My partner was not the problem, she just had a problem that needed to be solved. Now, this is the only time I will say that you can actually help solve a problem, mainly because I was directly involved with her life, romantically, and this problem would not have gone away had I left her at that moment. I decided that we would fix this problem together. She finally opened up to me about her abusive past and that her other friends had put a negative view on me. They were racist towards her being with me, a white American. Her friends had been pitting her to break up with me because like her, they too were Filipino. They believed in an old way of thinking, stick with your own race. This angered me.

I could not believe that she would betray our relationship for something so devious and destructive. I did not take it out on her though. I took it out on myself and my car. This scared her and it scared me too.

I loved this woman so much and still do today. I could not believe she would allow some outside force to come between our own relationship. My car had a small dent in the hood from contacting my fist, but that was not what hurt me the most. Her communication with me had been tarnished due to someone else interfering with our relationship. I know this was not how she truly felt, or she would never had agreed to be with me in the first place. When I finally calmed down, I reached back out to her and we agreed to meet up and talk. She was visibly upset at herself. She understood why I reacted the way I did. We began to talk about the issue at hand. She told me that the father of her first three kids was abusive towards her. He literally hit her on more than one occasion leaving scars that I did not even notice until she pointed them out. Violence is never the answer. You see, we all have scars; internally or externally. She has both and I was inconsiderate to not take notice to the visible ones. Not only did he physically abuse her, he mentally abused her by cheating on her on more than one occasion. This is where that insecurity started. The insecurity that was dragging our relationship to its knees.

After we finally talked about all of this we came to the point where the next chapter will take us, compromising. We were open and honest with each other and communicated our grievances. Our path forward would only be determined by our decision making and the next two chapters. She still has that insecurity, so it is still a work in progress. But it is not a problem like it was before.

Communicating our problems, needs, and wants is necessary to be open and honest with others.

When you establish trust, honesty, and communication you can begin to work on the last two keys. Communication must start with you as well. If you do not communicate, how can expect others to communicate with you as well?

If you are ready to start talking, which can be vocalized or visualized then say this:

*I (your name), will begin to communicate with the people in my relationships to foster trust and honesty. I will make sure that when I communicate that my needs and wants are clear and concise. I will maintain a good judgement and a productive mindset.*

# BARGAINING
# IN LIFE

As we begin to finalize our journey, there is a subject we must discuss thoroughly. We need to talk about compromising. It is a large part of everyday life. From our wants and needs to the wants and needs of others. We bargain almost every day. But, properly bargaining can be difficult to encompass in every relationship. There are individuals, in the collective world, that are part of a so-called "all or nothing" philosophical regime. Individuals, such as these, must be avoided. I mention this due to the nature of selfishness these specific individuals tend to harbor. If a person is selfish then there is an issue with ego. Having a large ego directs focus to only one person in a relationship. This is not only unfair but destructive as well. When we break down what compromising really means you will understand this.

Compromise is a joint word. 'Come' and 'together' are the breakdown of this word. When two or more individuals come to an agreement or an arrangement. It takes effort for those people to come together and decide on what appropriate actions must be taken together. To put it simply: it takes two to tango.

It is sufficient to say that compromising is an art. If you are a parent, you will know what I am talking about. With any kid you have to bargain with them on a constant basis. If I give you a cookie you have to clean your room. If you take out the trash, I will give you a couple dollars. This is bargaining in its simplest forms of understanding. We even do this as adults. Most people have jobs, these jobs are literally a compromise with a business for your services. The business hires you based on your skills and pays you a wage in return. You may not have noticed this but that is exactly a compromised deal. Either you have given enough information to a business for them to bet on your skills for financial compensation or you do not have what they are looking for in a candidate that will represent their mission and company.

In relationships, there is no need for an application per say. The application is usually a series of events and the previous mentioned attributes that count as the application process. If you trust someone then you eventually will get to this point of bargaining with them. Most compromises deal in time, some in money, while others in material items, but whatever the cost, both parties have to benefit from the bargain. If not, then the deal should be called off. Normally the benefit is building something as simple as a stronger relationship. A normal and fine agreement. (This is where that time portion comes into factor.) Every relationship is different, I get that, but every relationship requires sacrifice at some point. Being able to compromise is part of life. You sacrifice time, money, or material items to gain something in return which could be the same as mentioned.

Employment requires time and strength and in return you get financial gain. Friendships normally require listening and time, but you get a stronger relationship with someone that you can depend on if you were to ever need their help in the future.

Family is normally a given when it comes to sacrificing if you have a strong relationship already and normally gratitude is all you get in return Hopefully help from them as well in the future should you need it. Intimate relationships require the most bargaining.

Within the intimate relationship section of compromising, you need to understand that this can be tricky at some points to maneuver. Not everything you want will be what the other person wants. Not everything you need will be what the other person needs either. This is where communication is key in establishing a common goal. Once the common goal is decided then you can go into bargaining. You may not know you do this already since almost everyone does this so quickly. Sort of like marriage; if you marry me, I will marry you, if I pay for this bill you pay for the other bill. The list goes on.

For every relationship you either get something out of it or you cut ties with that individual. This entire understanding falls in line with the previous principals on maintaining relationships. If you cannot trust someone, why would you even want to bargain with them? All of these principals go hand in hand. You cannot have one without the other. I will give you a scenario.

My partner and I have our differences, which I am sure everyone does. We tend to disagree on certain aspects of life. For example: what we should buy for groceries. I know, it sounds childish, but you have to remember she is from a different country than I am, so our taste in food vary for the most part. When we first started dating, I never really liked trying new things not because I was afraid of change but because I liked what I liked and did not feel it was necessary to venture into new territory. Well, she ended up getting me to try a Filipino dish called dinuguan. Dinuguan is a simple dish.

It is made with pork and pork blood mainly but with some seasoning like vinegar, bay leaves, onion, garlic, and sugar to sweeten. At first, I thought this would never taste good at all. But we made a deal, a compromise. That compromise would consist of her having to ride a roller-coaster with me. She hates rollercoasters, like deathly afraid of them. We agreed and I tried it. I will tell you now, I loved it and it is one of my favorite Filipino dishes aside from lumpia. If you put those two together, you will not hear a peep from me the entire night.

In turn I never forgot about our arrangement and when a fair happened to come to town, she kept her end of the bargain and rode just one roller-coaster with me. It was the one that drops down a cylinder super-fast and stops right before the ground. She was jittery and nervous all the way up. She even closed her eyes the entire time as she screamed all the way down. Did I enjoy the food? You bet. Did she have fun as well? I would like to think so since she was also laughing and appeared to be having a good time as well.

You see, this is the kind of compromise that has to happen in relationships. It does not necessarily have to deal with monetary gain but instead it should mainly be upon getting the experience with someone you care about. That should be the end-goal. This is what life is anyway: a series of events that garner experience through relationships. Every single individual must care about the other person. Which leads us to the next key to a successful relationship. Before we move on, I want you to think about your past relationships and see where you had to make a compromise and how it turned out. Then say this:

*As I continue my journey in life, I will think of other's needs and wants and make compromises where both parties will be positively affected. I will learn from my experiences and apply what I have learned to every new relationship.*

# LOVE IS ALL
# YOU NEED

L ove is a tricky obstacle to avoid. As I have grown, I have come to the notion that there are two very different types of love and within the second one there is also two different types of it as well. Love is more than just a word; it is an emotional complex that drives most people. Love for what you do, love for mankind, love for animals, love for yourself, and love for another. To break this down, the basic realization is that love is either *platonic* or *intimate.*

Before we go into the two types, let's capture this moment to dive into the science behind the feeling of love. Phenylethylamine is a chemical naturally found in nature in the form of food and even within the brain. It is a reward stimulant in essence. When activated it releases dopamine, that good feeling, as well as norepinephrine which is a stress hormone.

When these chemicals are released, we get that feeling of love. Now with that out of the way let us dive into the different kinds of love.

Platonic love is a simple non-complex emotional response. It drives simple relationships; friendships, family, and even some of our desires to accomplish certain tasks in life like work. These formalities are simple because they do not require as much love in maintaining compared to the intimate love. Love is not just a word you can throw out there though. When we think of love as a term endearment it has multitudes of meaning. If you say it willingly, people can get the wrong impression and the word loses its power and meaning.

Kids are the most vulnerable to the term of love. We have to protect that understanding by ensuring that the term is not used in the wrong essence. Kids are sponges, after all. As they mature, kids tend to learn and identify how they feel with how it relates to the term of love. Saying 'I love you' to your kids is always a show of affection for their existence, but it is also platonic in nature. Adults must understand this to make sure there is no confusion for the child they are raising.

Personally, I do not throw love as a phrase to everyone I meet, due to my understanding of it. This usually happens to everyone eventually. Love can hurt but it can also heal. It all depends on how you use it.

Intimate love is the love between two partners. With this type of love, it is much stronger and has way more meaning to it. Intimate love requires even more sacrifice. Giving up loneliness is one of them. With each relationship prior to the intimacy between two partners, loneliness is a factor. When you have intimacy, you must bear in mind that your loneliness must be forgotten. Everything you do now must be thought out with the other person in mind. Decisions must be made together.

Within the scope of intimacy comes sexual desires and needs. We are a species that reproduces through sex, but we must also know the chemical rewards we get from love, mentioned earlier, includes the same as sexual activity. There are two kinds of sexual activity: creational and recreational. Most relations feel the need that sex is a requirement in a relationship with a partner. When broken down, the realization is that it is actually not completely true. If you want a child, then yes, by all means it is a requirement. But if your goal is deeper then it is not a requirement per say. Sex after childbirth, if another child is not wanted, becomes recreational. Same-sex relationships are recreational sexual relationships due to the non-factor of creation. As we age, our bodies change and sex becomes a sort of taboo subject. Unless there is a blue pill involved for men with erectile disfunction. Yes, I know, there's even a pill for women.

To clarify, sex does bring a relationship closer

because it breaks the wall of insecurity and loneliness. It is not the end of a relationship, because as you continue the relationship you have to maintain the previously mentioned staples of a relationship: trust, honesty, communication, and compromise. Sex is just part of intimate love, which is part of the larger meaning of love. Just try not to get mixed up in the language.

Love is strong due to passion. Love is enduring due to communication. It is sympathetic due to honesty. It trusts as well as compromises due to those we surround ourselves with. It is the strongest force in the universe, yet it is a huge secret and protected with a fortress. It is what makes us human and different compared to any other species. If you grasp this concept of understanding, then I want you to repeat this:

*I, (your name), am aware of the power of love. That it is a word yet also an emotional feeling that can heal but also destroy. I will use love to heal and nurture. I understand the complexity of what love for other entails and will be responsible in how I love others.*

# CONCLUSION

That was a lot to go through, but also very simple to understand, I hope. With every relationship we have in life; trust, honesty, communication, compromise, and love are essential in the foundations of maintaining them. It is not a one-way street. With every relationship, it must be wanted by more than one person. Otherwise, there is no relationship.

I can almost guarantee that you are asking why I did not include other points like respect, dignity, caring, or even understanding. If you really dig deep you will understand that all of these follow suit with the main five conceptional foundations of what is needed in a relationship. How can you love someone if they do not respect you? How can you care for someone if you do not trust them? Why would you make an effort in communication if you do not want to understand the other party's point of view? You see, this is why I wanted to bring awareness to the complications and theoretical concept of what a relationship needs in order to be successful.

With each of these concepts of basic relationship building you must first apply them to yourself. You have to be able to trust your decision making. You must be able to be honest with what your needs and wants are in life. You need to communicate in order to be understood. Within your personal life, you need to be able to compromise certain aspects in order to achieve your end-goal. Lastly, you have to love yourself as a human being that is part of a bigger picture. It takes time on that last one, to be honest, but it is pivotal in being able to have a relationship with someone else.

You may be wondering; how did I figure this out? It was not easy. I went through many trials as well as heartbreaks with many family members, friends, and even in my intimate relationships. It took me almost 10 years to figure it out. 10 years is a long time and I hope no one has to endure that much time to figure it outlike I did. That's why I wrote this book; for people like yourself to know what love has to do with it among the other keys. If it has taken 10 years to figure it out, please accept my mutual apology. No one should have to go through that much pain when knowledge is power that is widely accessible in today's world.

With this book, I hope that you can build new relationships, repair broken ones, and maintain them for years to come. Share what you have learned. By hiding knowledge that benefits everyone, we harbor a selfish mindset that only hurts others. If you ever feel that you need a refresher course, just pick this book back up and re-read it. Be mindful of others. Remember, to have a successful relationship you need to utilize all five keys: trust, honesty, communication, compromise, and love.

# ABOUT THE AUTHOR

## N. J. Dicarlo

I served in the US Army as a 91S, which is a Stryker Systems Maintainer.

I am a creative writer, blogger, and screenwriter.

My first written work was on an old Windows 2000 OS Dell with the big white boxed monitor at the age of maybe 12. I've lost it since then but I still remember what it was about. Since then, I've written lyrics for songs, written multiple feature film scripts, and written for theatre. Now I can say I am a self-published author. Needless to say, it has been a journey.

Made in the USA
Middletown, DE
08 August 2021

45160510R00031